Oboe Fingering and Scale Chart

By Eric Nelson

MEL BAY®

Fingering Chart: Oboe

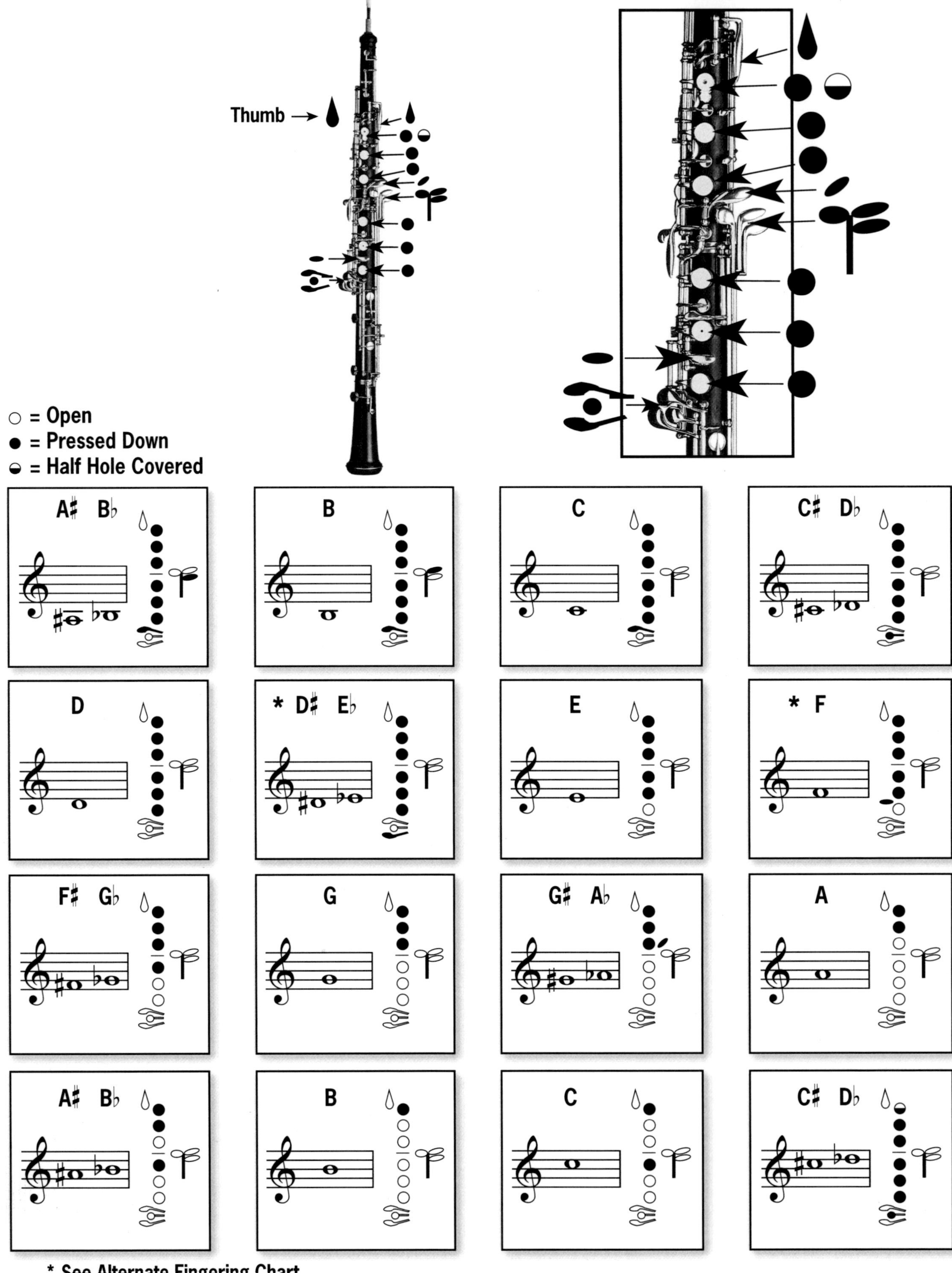

* See Alternate Fingering Chart